CONTENTS

INTRODUCTION

If you've ever wanted to know what it feels like to drive or sail some of the most extreme boats in the world then *The Need for Speed* will show you.

This book features the whole range of high-adrenaline high-speed boat experiences. Strap yourself into the cockpit of a powerboat, as you blast through deadly waves at over 241km/h (150mph). Brave the world's roughest waters and strongest winds in a tough and powerful ocean racer. Then maybe relax in luxury aboard the incredible Predator motoryacht and let someone else do the driving!

As well as the thrills and spills, we also give you the facts and figures behind these incredible machines. For most types of boat featured there is a Stat File and a Fact File.

This line tells you the model of boat used as an example.

These lines give details about such things as engine size, acceleration and top speed.

The technical terms used in this book are explained on page 31.

STAT FILE

Outlaw Sportboat

Weight	400kg (882lbs)
Length	4.55m (15ft)
Beam	1.8m (6ft)
Acceleration	0-74km/h in 10 secs
Engine	95Hp
Top speed	74km/h (46mph)
Crew	2-4

The Fact File gives a slightly unusual, strange or funny bit of information about the boat.

FACT FILE

It doesn't matter if you live a long way from the sea. Sportsboats are small enough to keep in the garden and light enough to tow behind a car on a trailer.

Yellow Pages
ENDEAVOUR

RONSTAN BOTE COTE
CSIRO CLUB MARINE
HONDA SP Systems
ANL SWAN HAR

Yellow Pages
ENDEAVOUR

CLASS 1 POWERBOATS

Class 1 powerboats are the fastest racing boats in the world. Two massive engines drive these spectacular machines at up to 241km/h (150mph), which is twice as fast as a car on a motorway. A team of experts look after each boat and its engines. Racing a Class 1 boat costs a lot of money – more than half a million pounds a year.

Powerboat engines can be bigger than aeroplane engines. They take up half the space in the boat and have the same pulling power as nine hundred horses. As the boat blasts off, the engines create a huge wake and makes a tremendous roar, which can be heard far out to sea. Powerboat racing is a very noisy sport!

Class 1 powerboats have two crew. There is one person to steer and one to adjust the speed. These boats race far away from the shore, where waves can be high enough to flip a boat over. To protect themselves, the crew sit in an enclosed cockpit. It is made of specially strong plastic, the same material used in a fighter jet cockpit.

There are many teams involved in powerboat racing, all of them trying to develop a boat that will beat the rest. This means that the boats all look different.

Class 1 Powerboat

Weight of boat without engine	2 tonnes
Weight of boat with engine	4.5 tonnes
Length	15m (48ft)
Width	3m (10ft)
Engine	2 x 9000Hp
Fuel consumption	1.6km (1 mile) per gallon (a family car does 56km (35 miles) per gallon)
Hull	Wood & GRP (glass reinforced plastic)
Crew	2
Race range	61-257km (100-160 miles)
Average racing speed	225km/h (140mph)
Fastest record	251km/h (156mph)

Races

The races are about 257km (160 miles) long. The boats compete around large inflatable buoys. Powerboat racing is very dangerous, so rescue teams follow the race from above in helicopters. If a boat crashes, the helicopter throws down a line to the crew and pulls them out of the water.

Class 2 powerboats look similar to those in Class 1 but are slightly smaller. There are two different styles of Class 2 boats – monohulls, which have one hull and catamarans, which have two hulls.

A monohull cuts right through the waves, while a catamaran rides on a cushion of air between the two hulls. This lifts the boat up above the waves and makes it look as if it is flying. The catamarans win when the water is flat, but monohulls triumph when conditions are bumpy.

The catamarans have two 600 horse power engines and can reach speeds of 209km/h (130mph). Monohulls have only one 800 horse power engine and reach speeds of up to 193km/h (120mph).

If a boat hits a monster wave at top speed it may even break in half and sink. To keep safe, the crew wear waterproof survival suits, life jackets and crash helmets.

The crew must talk to each other all the time while they are racing, but it's hard to hear anything above the noisy engines. They speak using walkie-talkies fitted inside their helmets.

STAT FILE

Class 2 Powerboat

Weight of boat without engine	2 1/4 tonnes
Length	11m (36ft)
Width catamarans	3m (10ft)
Width monohulls	2.4m (8ft)
Engine catamarans	2 x 600Hp
Engine monohulls	1 x 800Hp
Fuel consumption	2.4km (1.5 miles) per gallon
Hull	Wood & GRP (glass reinforced plastic)
Crew	2
Race range	161km (100 miles)
Race speed Catamarans	209km/h (130mph)
Race speed Monohulls	193km/h (120mph)

FACT FILE

Sponsorship

Powerboating is very expensive, so the crews usually ask sponsors to help pay for the boat and fuel. In return, the sponsors put the name of their companies on the side of the boat for everyone to see.

CIRCUIT RACING POWERBOATS

Circuit racing powerboats are much smaller than Class 1 and Class 2 powerboats, but they still travel across the water at a fantastic 209km/h (130mph). You only need one driver, called a pilot, and a large lake to race on. Turning when it reaches the end of the lake is no problem for a circuit racing boat – it can turn a tight corner at 145km/h (90mph)! The G-force on the pilot's body when turning at such speed is greater than the G-force on a pilot in a fighter jet. It's a very tough sport.

Circuit races have very short triangular courses, so the pilots have to go round up to 65 times in one race. Unlike offshore Class 1 & 2 powerboat racing, circuit racing is close to land so people can watch. A fleet of 24 boats line up side by side in front of the crowds. When the starter's gun fires, they scream away to the first buoy. It's very exciting for both the pilots and the spectators! There's always plenty of action. When 24 boats are racing together at 209km/h (130mph), the crowd are sure to see lots of capsizes and crashes.

Powerboat Speak

Here are some terms that powerboaters use to describe the hazards of their sport:

A Barrel-roll: when a boat leaves the water and does a somersault at high speed.

A Hook: when a boat suddenly turns sharply to the left or right. A hook can easily throw a crew member into the water.

A Spin Out: when a boat goes too fast round a corner and jumps out of the water.

A Stuff: when a boat dives completely under the water. This can only happen at full speed.

A Trip: when a boat takes off from a wave and lands nose first, usually ending in a stuff.

STAT FILE

Circuit Racing Powerboat

Weight of boat without engine	3/4 tonnes (Same weight as a small car)
Length	6m (20ft)
Width	2.28m (7.6ft)
Engine	1 x 395Hp
Fuel consumption	136ltr (30 gallons)
Hull	Wood & GRP (glass reinforced plastic)
Crew	1
Acceleration	0-97km/h in 5.8 seconds
Top speed	209km/h (130mph)

FACT FILE

Circuit racing boats accelerate faster than any other craft. Over 50m (165ft) they accelerate almost as fast as a Formula One racing car.

SKIFF DINGHY

Skiffs are great fun to race! A Skiff's hull is very small and light, but it carries enormous, powerful sails, which makes it extremely fast. Skiffs are difficult to sail and the three man crew have to be very active to keep the boat upright. Everybody has an important job to do. The front person controls the jib, the middle person is in charge of the mainsail and the back person steers, or helms.

Skiffs are very unstable. They have to keep moving to stay upright, other wise they fill up with water and capsize. Watching Skiff racing is always action packed as the crews struggle to balance their boats.

To carry such a large spinnaker sail, the Skiff has a extra long pole coming out of the front of the boat. This is called a bowsprit. To balance the weight of the wind in the sails, the crew leans out on the boat's wings.

Crew on wing

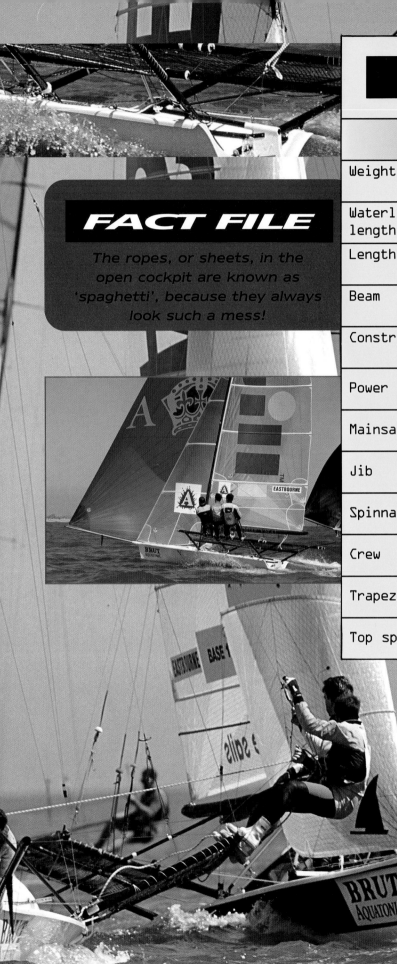

STAT FILE

Ultra-Light Skiff

Weight	130kg (287lbs) (The weight of two adults)
Waterline length	5.48m (18ft) (with bowsprit and rudders)
Length overall	10m (33ft) (with bowsprit and rudders)
Beam	1.82m (6ft) without wings 5.82m (19ft) with wings
Construction	super light-weight kevlar and carbon fibre
Power	3 sails
Mainsail	17m² (183ft²)
Jib	9m² (97ft²)
Spinnaker	60m² (646ft²)
Crew	3
Trapezes	3
Top speed	55km/h (34mph)

FACT FILE

The ropes, or sheets, in the open cockpit are known as 'spaghetti', because they always look such a mess!

The wings make the Skiff as wide as it is long, forcing the crew to hang high in the air as they fly along at speeds of up to 55km/h (34mph). To do this they are supported by a thin wire, called a trapeze, which attaches to each crew member by a special harness.

SPORTS CATAMARAN

A Hawk is the fastest type of sports catamaran. Like all catamarans, it has two long, thin hulls, but spends most of the time with one hull high in the air. When a Hawk accelerates, the whole boat tips onto one side, lifting the two crew right out of the water. This is called flying a hull, and it's the most exciting way to sail a catamaran. In very strong winds the crew can be standing 3m (10ft) in the air!

Sailing a Hawk is a fast, wet ride and it's exhausting for the crew. They must try to keep the hull flying just above the water, which is not always easy.

A catamaran needs two rudders. If one comes out of the water, the helm can steer the boat with the other. The helm uses an extra long tiller for moving the rudders while hanging way out on a trapeze.

The Hawk has three sails, but there are only two crew. This means the front crew member has to control the spinnaker and the jib at the same time. The helm controls the mainsail with one hand and steers the boat with the other.

STAT FILE

Sports Catamaran

Length	5.5m (18ft) with Bowsprit & rudder
Beam	2.6m (8.5ft)
Hull	Wood & GRP (glass reinforced plastic)
Sail area	42m² (452ft²)
Mainsail	17m² (183ft²)
Jib	4.4m² (47ft²)
Genoa	21.8m² (235ft²)
Crew	2
Top speed	55km/h (34mph)

Rudder

FACT FILE

When the crew change from one side of the boat to the other, they have to quickly crawl across a soft trampoline that stretches across the middle of the boat.

OCEAN RACING YACHT

An ocean racer is the fastest type of monohull yacht. It is so tough and powerful, it can cope with the world's roughest oceans and strongest winds. It normally has a large mainsail at the back, and a smaller sail at the bow, called the Genoa, or jib. When the wind is blowing behind the boat, the crew put up an extra, massive sail, called a spinnaker. It quickly fills up with wind and pushes the boat even faster. The fastest ocean racing yachts can cover over 644km (400 miles) in 24 hours.

When sailing downwind, an ocean racer can reach breathtaking top speeds of 45km/h (28mph).

The sails on an ocean racing yacht are far too large and heavy to move by hand so the crew use winches to sheet them in and out.

In strong winds, an ocean racing yacht can heel right over on its side. But, unlike a small sailing dinghy, it cannot actually capsize. The heavy keel on the bottom of the hull always pulls the boat upright again.

Ocean Racing Yacht

Weight overall	13.5 tonnes
Keel	8 tonnes (including 5 tonnes of lead in the bulb)
Length	19.5m (64ft)
Width	5.25m (17ft)
Hull	Kevlar
Mast	29m (95ft)
Power	3 Sails
Sail area	220–500m^2 (2368–5382ft^2)
Draught	3.7m^2 (40ft^2)
Average crew	12
Top speed	55km/h (34mph)

FACT FILE

The hulls on ocean racing yachts are made of a super-light material called Kevlar. It's so strong, it's also used to make bullet-proof jackets.

Every 4 years about 12 ocean racing yachts race each other around the world in the Whitbread Round the World Race. This is the toughest of all sailing races. It lasts 8 months and the yachts race over 50,854km (31,600 miles) from start to finish.

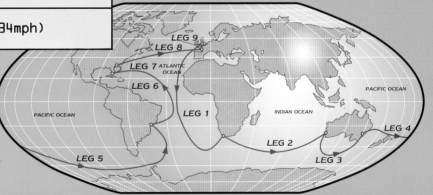

The course - The Whitbread Round The World Race 1997-98

LEG 1	LEG 2	LEG 3	LEG 4	LEG 5	LEG 6
Southampton to Cape Town 11,828 nautical km	Cape town to Fremantle 7,403 nautical km	Fremantle to Sydney 3,621 nautical km	Sydney to Auckland 2,044 nautical km	Auckland to Sao Sebastiao 10,734 nautical km	Sao Sebastiao to Fort Launderale 1,400 nautical km

LEG 7	LEG 8	LEG 9
Fort Lauderdale to Baltimore 7,644 nautical km	Annapolis to La Rochelle 5,456 nautical km	La Rochelle to Southampton 724 nautical km

Total race distance of approximately 50,854 nautical km

OCEAN RACING CATAMARAN

Ocean racing 'cats' are the biggest of catamarans and the fastest of all sailing boats. These are mean racing machines capable of sailing non-stop around the world. It takes lots of crew to race a boat this big and fast. In rough weather they attach themselves to the guard rails with safety clips, to stop being thrown over-board.

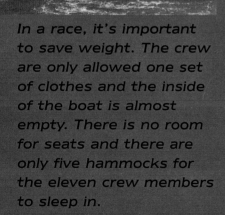

An ocean racing catamaran goes much faster than a monohull yacht because it's longer, wider and carries bigger sails. It's so stable, it never tips or heels over, even in the roughest weather.

In a race, it's important to save weight. The crew are only allowed one set of clothes and the inside of the boat is almost empty. There is no room for seats and there are only five hammocks for the eleven crew members to sleep in.

Races around the world take up to 80 days, which can be lonely. The crew use computers and satellite phones to let rescue teams and families know that they are okay.

FACT FILE

There is no fresh water on board, so the crew use a special machine that turns the sea into drinking water. There is no fresh food either. When the crew want to eat, they mix packets of dried food with the specially made water. School food never sounded so good!

STAT FILE

Ocean Racing Catamaran

Weight	9.75 tonnes
Length	28m
Beam	12.8m (42ft)
Hull	Kevlar (same bullet proof material as their sails)
Mast height	32m (105ft)
Sail area	610m² (6566ft²)
Crew	11
Top speed	63km/h (39mph)

Round the world records

Lots of people try to break the speed record for sailing around the world in ocean racing cats. Not everybody makes it. All the pictures on this page show the Royal & Sun Alliance attempting the record. Sadly the mast snapped after 30 days at sea and the all-female crew had to return home.

YELLOW PAGES ENDEAVOUR

The owners of this boat never take it out just for a fun sail at the weekend. It is purely for smashing speed records. In 1993, the Yellow Pages Endeavour beat the world sailing speed record by sailing at an incredible 85km/h (53mph). Unlike normal boats, Endeavour doesn't have a hull. It sits on feet called hydrofoils, which keep the yacht afloat.

The hydrofoils are one of the reasons why Endeavour travels so fast. Most sailing boats have large hulls which push against the water and this slows them down. Endeavour's mini feet rise up above the water and skim lightly across the surface. Although the vessel is 12m (39ft) long, only a tiny part touches the water.

Most sailing boats have several soft sails that fill with wind. Endeavour has one solid wing, like an aeroplane's wing standing on its end. This makes the boat quicker, but the sail is fixed and can't swing round. Unlike normal sailing boats, Endeavour can only sail in one direction!

The crew are crouched up in a tiny bubble cockpit on the end of a pole. They are suspended high in the air and balance against the giant wing to keep the flying machine upright. It's a very scary ride!

Yellow Pages Endeavour	
Weight	190kg (419lbs)
Length	10.8m (35ft)
Beam	10.8m (35ft)
Hull	Plywood reinforced with glass fibre
Mast height	12m (39ft)
Wing area	21–28m² (225–305ft²)
Crew	2
Official top speed	85km/h (53mph)

It took Endeavour several attempts to break the world speed record. It could not turn round, so it kept having to be towed back along the 500-m (1640-ft) course to have another go.

For five years, windsurfers kept breaking the world sailing speed record. Nothing else could beat them. Then came Endeavour! It broke the record by finishing the same course just 4km/h (2.5mph) faster than the smaller windsurfers.

FACT FILE

Endeavour really is faster than the wind! When it broke the record, it was travelling at 85km/h (53mph), and the wind was only blowing at 34km/h (21mph)!

PREDATOR MOTORYACHT

Imagine going for a ride in this amazing dream boat. It's designed to take you wherever you want to go at great speed and in total luxury.

The Predator has a hull like a racing boat, but inside, it's a grand palace with lavishly furnished rooms. Only a few Predators are made each year and they are very expensive, so only the rich can afford them.

As you can see, the inside of the Predator is not like a boat. It's more like a beautiful hotel. While the captain drives the boat, you can lie on one of the big sofas and watch TV!

The deck is so high out of the water, you can lie in the sun and stay dry as the Predator charges through the waves.

This is where the captain sits to drive the boat. He uses the wheel to steer and moves the throttles to speed up or slow down. There are also computers, satellite telephones and radar to help navigate. When the weather is good, you can even open the sun roof.

STAT FILE

Predator Motoryacht

Weight	49,000kg (108,025lbs) (the weight of 50 family cars)
Length	24m (79ft)
Beam	6m (20ft)
Fuel capacity	6000ltr (1320 gallons)
Range	644km (400 miles)
Fresh water	1025ltr (225 gallons)
Hull	GRP
Cruising speed	66km/h (41mph)
Top speed	77km/h (48mph)
Acceleration	0-55km/h in 25 secs 0-74km/h in 40 seconds
Sleeps	8
Crew	2

FACT FILE

There is a smaller version of the Predator motoryacht, called the Tomahawk. You can see it in Spice Girls – The Movie.

The Predator has another boat hidden inside it. A door flips down and releases a tender called the Bandit! This little boat carries people from the Predator into a small harbour or on to the beach.

23

SEACAT FERRY

SeaCat is the fastest passenger ferry in the world. Every day it carries hundreds of people and their cars across the Channel between England and France. It has two long, thin hulls made of light aluminium metal, which help it to go twice as fast as an ordinary ferry.

As the huge SeaCat speeds along, powerful waterjet engines lift the twin hulls high above the water and give passengers a smooth ride, even in very rough weather.

To reach its top speed of 77km/h (48mph), massive diesel engines spin at 750 times per minute, sucking water into the waterjets, and then blasting the water back out again. This creates a monster wake.

To steer in harbours, the bow is fitted with a bow thruster to help the captain squeeze SeaCat into tight moorings.

SeaCat uses the latest computerised navigation equipment, but on the bridge, they still have a crew member with binoculars to keep a look-out for smaller boats in the crowded Channel!

Record breaker!

In 1990, the first SeaCat ever built, 'Hoverspeed Great Britain', broke a world speed record on its maiden voyage.

It won the Blue Riband for the fastest crossing of the Atlantic between New York USA and Cornwall in the UK.

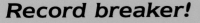

SeaCat Ferry

Weight	3003 tonnes (the weight of 1500 Rolls-Royce Cars)
Length	73.6m (241ft)
Beam	6.3m (86ft)
Hull shape	Catamaran
Hull construction	Aluminium
Power	4 diesels producing 3600 kilowatts of energy (enough power for 90,000 light bulbs)
Average crew	20
Passengers	up to 600
Car capacity	80
Draught	2.5m (8ft) when fully loaded
Top speed	77km/h (48mph)

FACT FILE

SeaCats were designed by the same Italian company that shaped some of the world's most famous sports cars, such as Ferrari and Alfa Romeo.

25

SPORTSBOAT

A sportsboat is small, light, easy to drive and great fun. There are no cabins to sleep in and there is no roof so you can't travel long distances or go out in rough weather. But it's ideal for speeding about close to the shore.

The boat bounces and zigzags through the waves as it zooms along, so passengers must hold on tight.

The sportsboat in this picture is called the Outlaw. It accelerates from a stand-still faster than any family car. As it reaches a top speed of 74km/h (46mph), you really feel the rush of wind in your face. It's like being on a roller coaster ride.

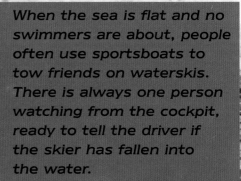

When the sea is flat and no swimmers are about, people often use sportsboats to tow friends on waterskis. There is always one person watching from the cockpit, ready to tell the driver if the skier has fallen into the water.

Outlaw Sportsboat

Weight	400kg (882lbs)
Length	4.55m (15ft)
Beam	1.8m (6ft)
Acceleration	0-74km/h in 10 secs
Engine	95Hp
Top speed	74km/h (46mph)
Crew	2-4

It doesn't matter if you live a long way from the sea. Sportsboats are small enough to keep in the garden and light enough to tow behind a car on a trailer.

Most sportsboats have an outboard engine, which fixes onto the stern (left). The Bandit (main picture) uses a jet engine which sucks water in, then forces it out again. The power of the water shooting out pushes the boat forwards.

VSV WAVE PIERCER

Wave Piercer is a unique boat. Waves cannot slow it down or damage it. Unlike all other boats which ride on the top of the water, Wave Piercer can duck underneath without losing speed. It's made of the strongest materials, so even the biggest waves can't break it and it carries enough fuel to blast for ten hours non-stop. So who wants a boat like this?

The Wave Piercer is used for special military assignments, because it's difficult to spot. The thin silver and white hull is almost invisible as it speeds across the horizon, and it sits so low in the water, even Radars find it hard to pick up. You'd be lucky to ever see one of these boats!

Wave Piercer

Weight	7340kg (16,182lbs) (the weight of about 100 adults)
Length	16m (53ft) (same length as a coach)
Beam	2.86m (9ft)
Draught	1m (3ft)
Engines	2 x 660hp
Fuel tank	3000 ltrs (660 gallons (3000 large bottles of Coca-Cola)
Range	805km (500 miles) (England to Scotland on one fuel tank)
Speed	92km/h (57mph)

When Wave Piercer is lifted out of the water, you can see how skinny the hull looks. This needle-like shape helps the boat shoot through the waves, making Wave Piercer very fast indeed.

The two crew sit in a sealed cockpit. They are completely safe in here. Even if Wave Piercer turns upside down, it automatically flips back upright again.

There is just enough room in the cockpit for the crew and all their hi-tech equipment, including a Radar screen, speedometer, compass, computerised maps and a depth sounder that tells the crew how deep the water is.

FACT FILE

When the Wave Piercer travels at its top speed of 92 km/h (57mph), it may completely submerge. You could say it's more like a submarine than a boat!

If you want to get involved in some of the water sports mentioned in this book, either to watch or to actually take part, here are some names and numbers that might be useful.

Associations, Classes & Manufacturers
UK

Royal Yachting Association
Tel: 01703 627400
Governing body for: Skiffs
Ocean Racing Yachts
Ocean Racing Catamarans
Powerboats - Class 1 Class 2
and Formula 1
World Speed Sailing Association

Predator Motor Yacht &
Outlaw Sports Boats
Sunseeker International Ltd
27-31 West Quay Road
Poole
Dorset
BH15 1HX
Tel: 01202 381111

Skiff Association
Tel: 0171 610 9506

SeaCat Hoverspeed
Tel: 01304 865162

Dart Catamaran Laser Centre
Tel: 01295 268191

Magazines, Books & Videos

Race Boat International Magazine
Tel: 01202 778658
Powerboats - Class 1 Class 2
and Formula 1

Yachts & Yachting Magazine
196 Eastern Esplanade
Southend on Sea
Essex SS1 3AB
Tel: 01702 582245

Skiffs, Ocean Racers and Catamarans
Ocean Leisure
11/14 Northumberland Ave
London WC2N 5AQ
Tel: 0171 930 5050
Retail, magazines, books & videos

Where to see

The Royal Yachting Association has race calendars for most yachting and power boating events in the UK.

The International London Boat Show is held every January at Earls Court in London.

The Southampton Boat Show is held every September.

TECHNICAL TERMS

There are some words in this book which you may not have seen before. Here is an explanation of them.

Buoy: floating marker to tie up to, or turn around.

Bowsprit: a pole sticking out from the front of the boat.

Bow-thruster: extra propeller at the bow to help steer big boats.

'Cats': nickname for catamarans.

Capsize: when a boat turns over.

Catamarans: two-hulled boat.

Craft: type of boat.

Downwind: sailing with the wind behind you.

Dinghy: small sailing boat.

Draught: the depth of water needed to float a ship.

Fleet: group or gathering of boats.

Flying a hull: when a hull comes out of the water.

Genoa: larger version of a jib.

GRP: glass reinforced plastic.

Gybing: turning a sailing boat around away from the wind.

Harbour: where boats are kept.

Heels or heeling: when a boat tips on its side.

Helm: person who steers the boat.

Horse power: a measurement of engine power.

Jet engine: engine which forces water out for speed instead of using a propeller.

Jib: small sail at the front of the boat.

Keel: heavy weight at the bottom of the boat to stop it falling over.

Knots: term used to measure the speed of a boat (7 knots is the same as 8 miles per hour).

Life jackets: jackets to help the crew float in the water in the case of a accident.

Liner: a large passenger ship.

Maiden Voyage: a boat's first journey.

Monohulls: single-hulled boats.

Moored/Moorings: when a boat is tied up to a buoy or anchored in a bay.

Navigate: deciding the course of the boat.

Offshore: a long way out to sea.

Outboard: engine fixed on the back of a boat.

RPM: revolutions per minute – the number of times something turns a complete circle in a minute.

Sheet: a rope or the action of pulling on a rope.

Spinnaker: a large extra sail at the bow of a boat.

Sponsors: people who pay to put their name on a boat.

Steer: control the direction of the boat.

Submarine: a ship that can operate underwater.

Tacking: turning a sailing boat into the wind.

Tender: smaller boat used to transfer passengers to the land.

Tiller: handle used to move the rudder.

Throttles: levers that control the speed.

Torpedo: long thin missile.

Trampoline: canvas area for the crew to move across.

Trapeze: wire from the top of the mast for crew to hang off.

Wake: foamy water behind the boat.

Waterline length: length of the boat touching the water.

Winch: machine to help the crew pull on the ropes.

Windward: the side on which the wind blows.

Wings: metal bars to make the boat wider.

INDEX